Easter & S... COLORING
BOOK FOR TODDLERS

AGES 1-4+

Big & Easy Pictures to Color

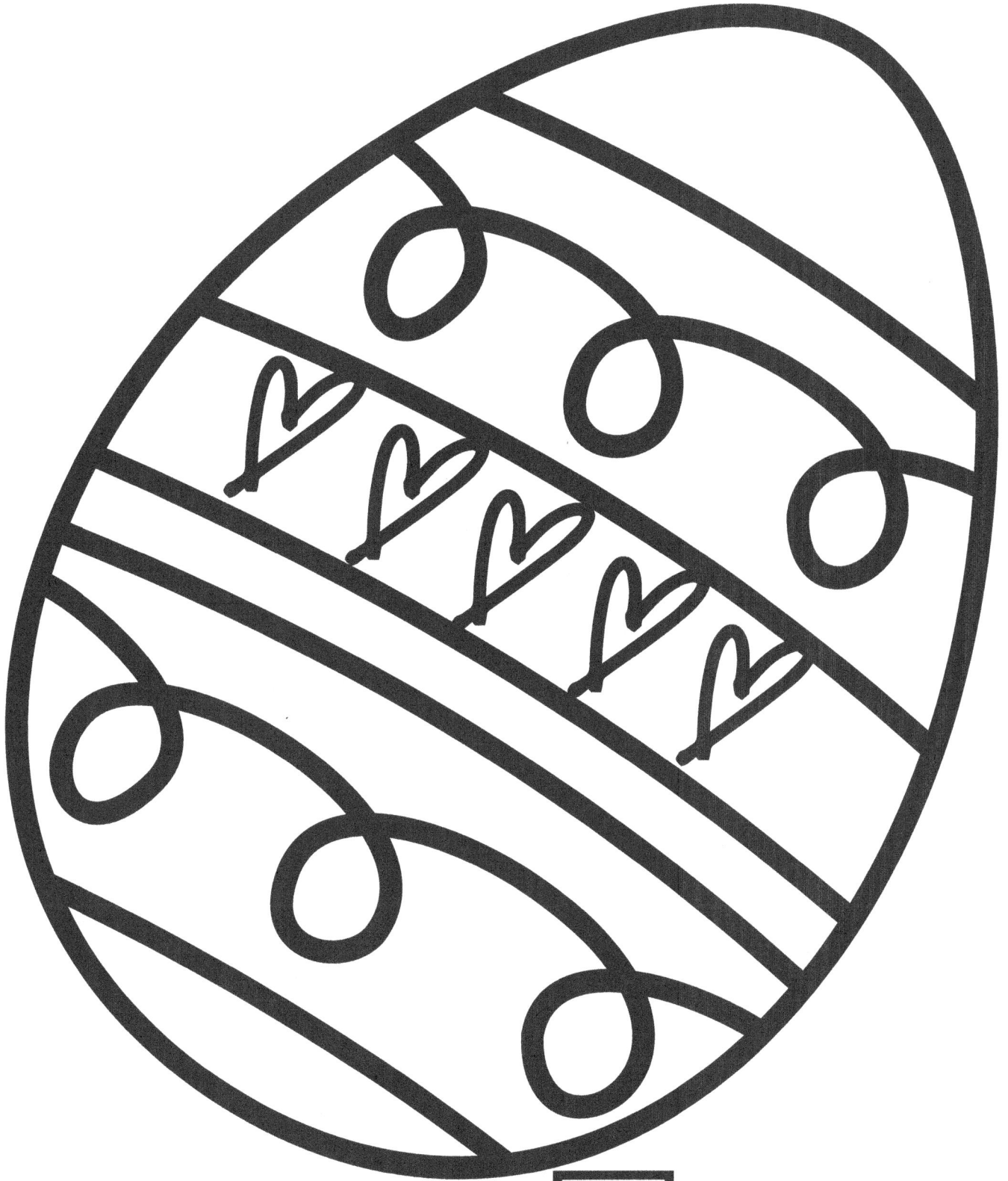

Egg

Chick

Bouquet

Bunny

Basket

Carrot

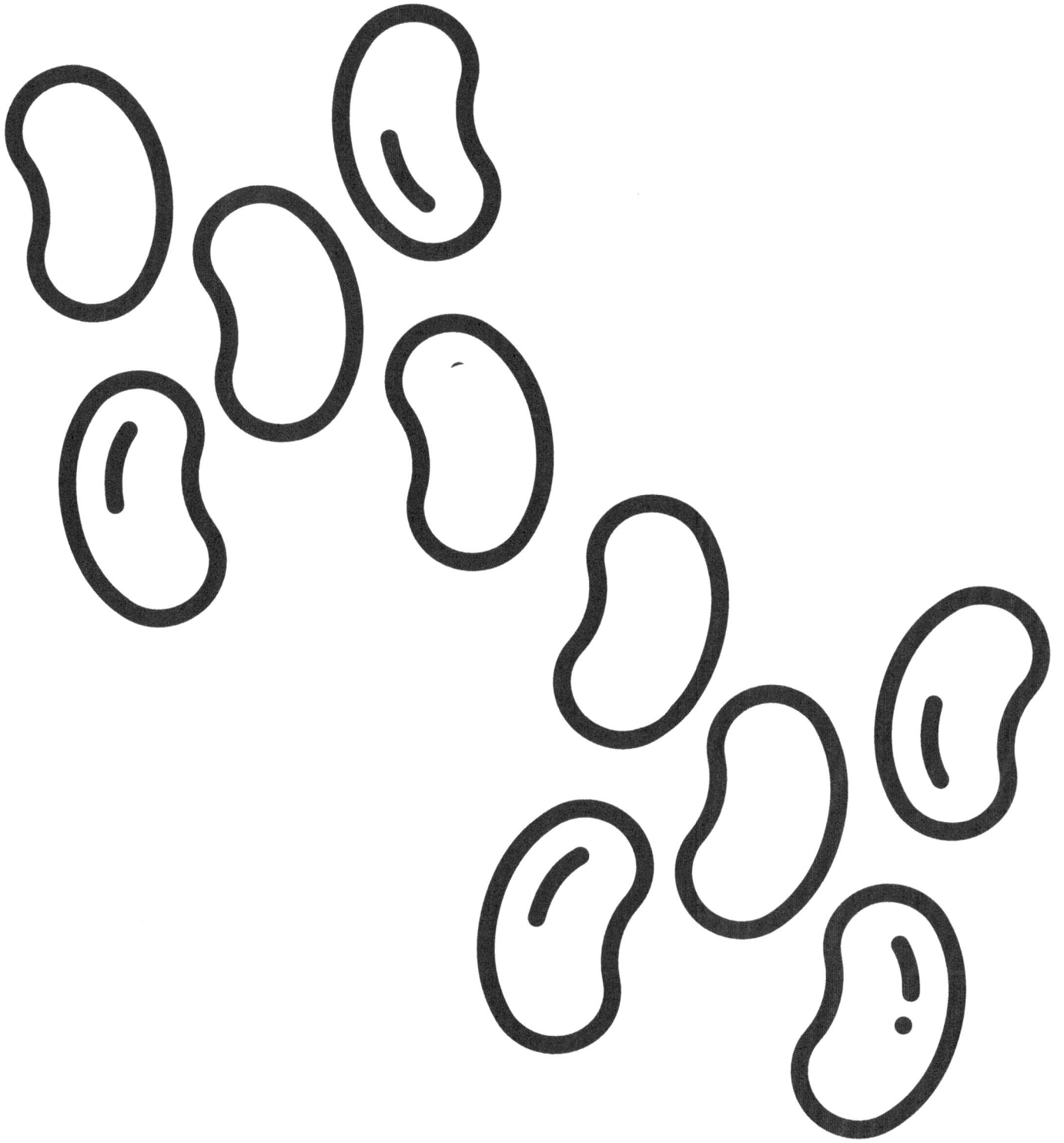

Jelly Beans

Cupcake

Rabbit

Tulip

Bunny

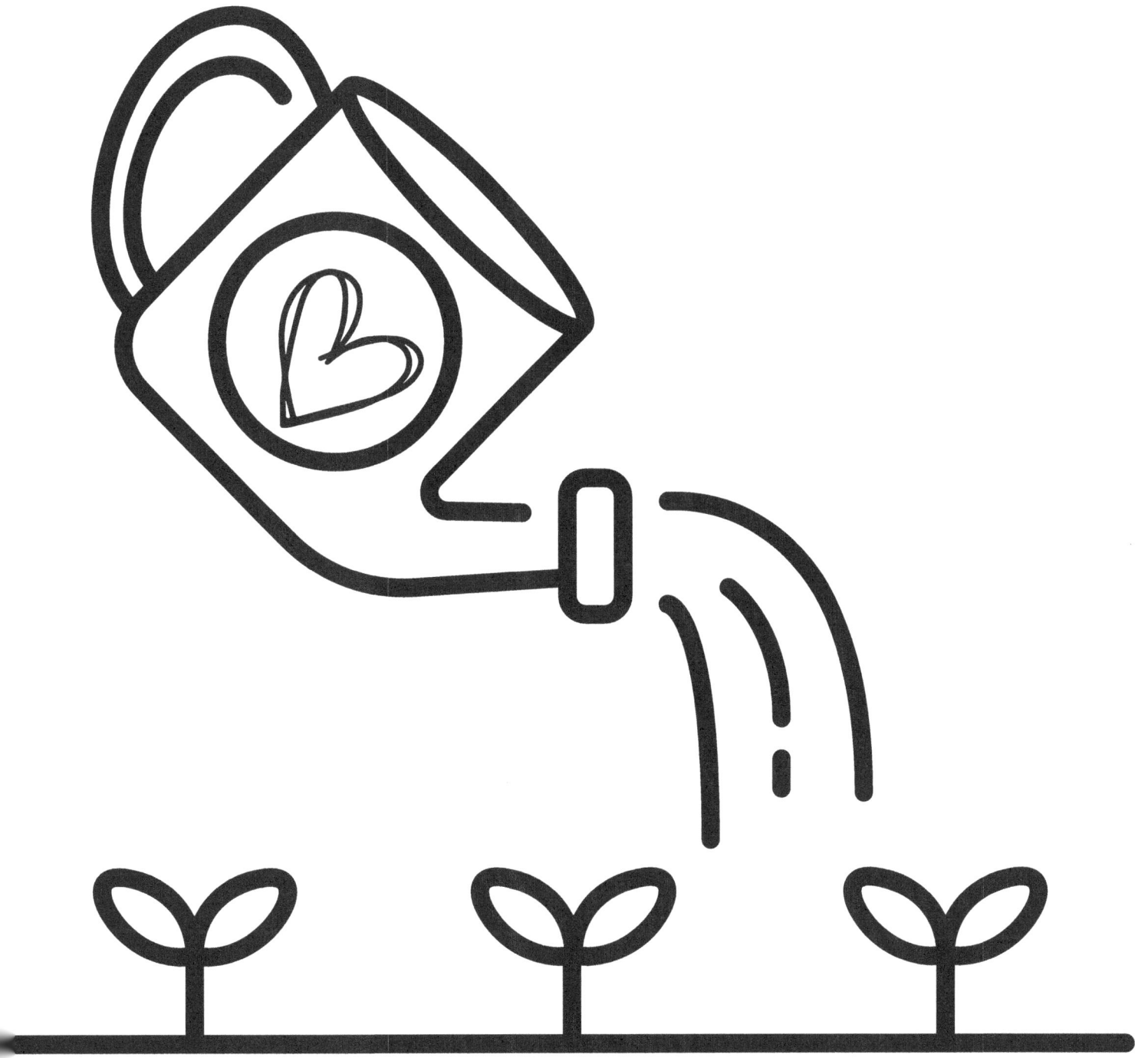

Seedlings

Umbrella

Nest

Strawberry

Lily

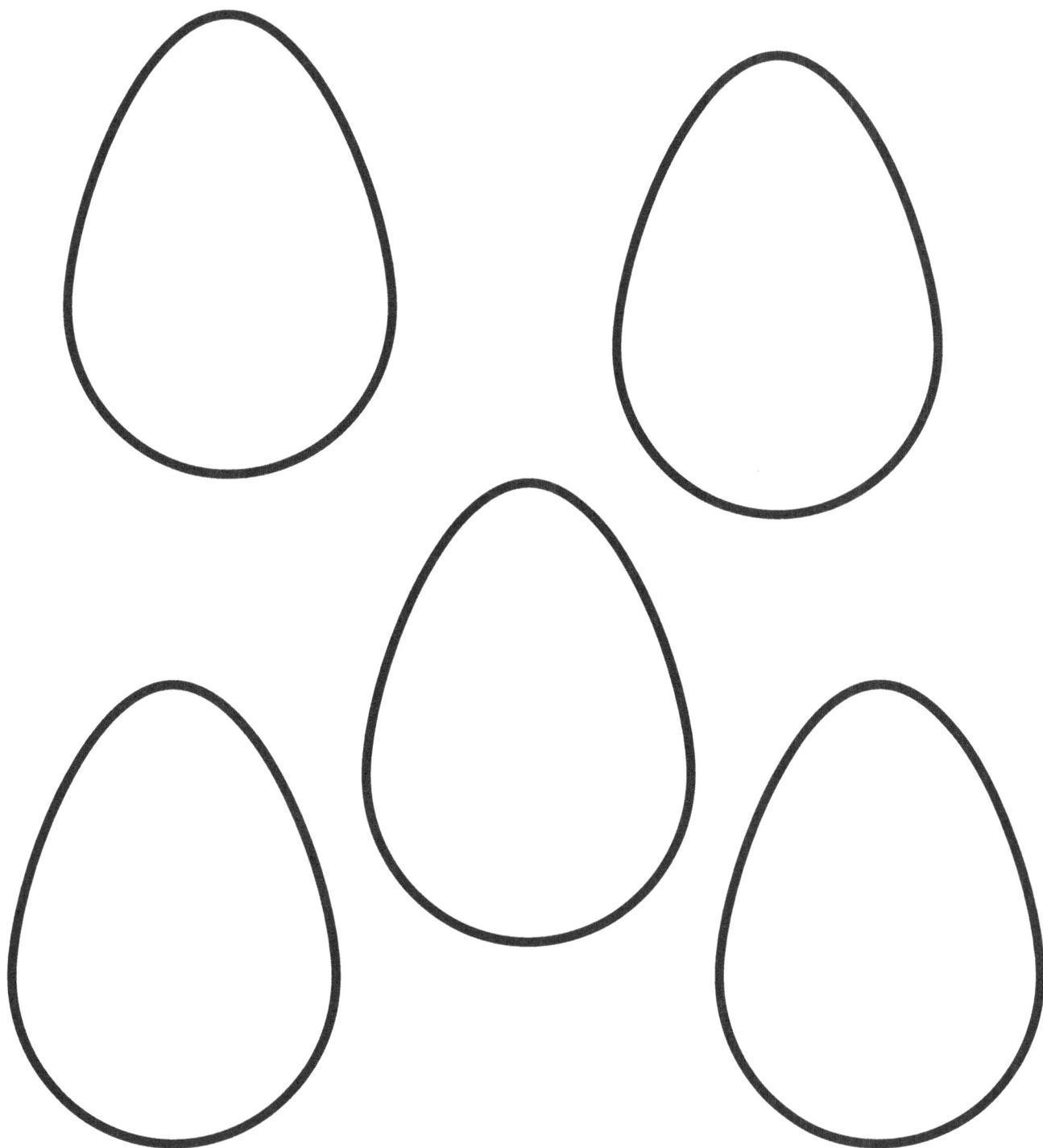

Eggs

Hen

Daffodil

Bees

Easter Basket

Sunshine

Bunny

Lamb

Flower Garden

Caterpillar

Rain

Bunny

Rainbow

Egg Hunt

Tree Blossoms

Easter Basket

Easter Bunny

Hop

Garden Gloves

Watering Can

Garden
Box

Fence

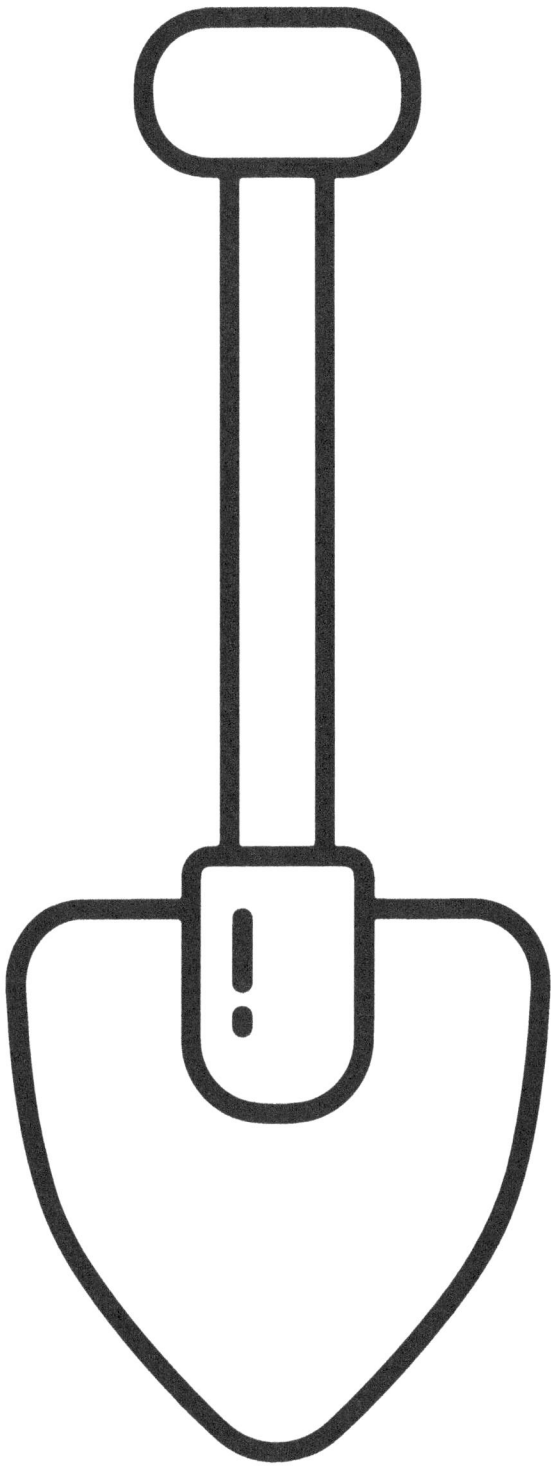

Shovel

Egg

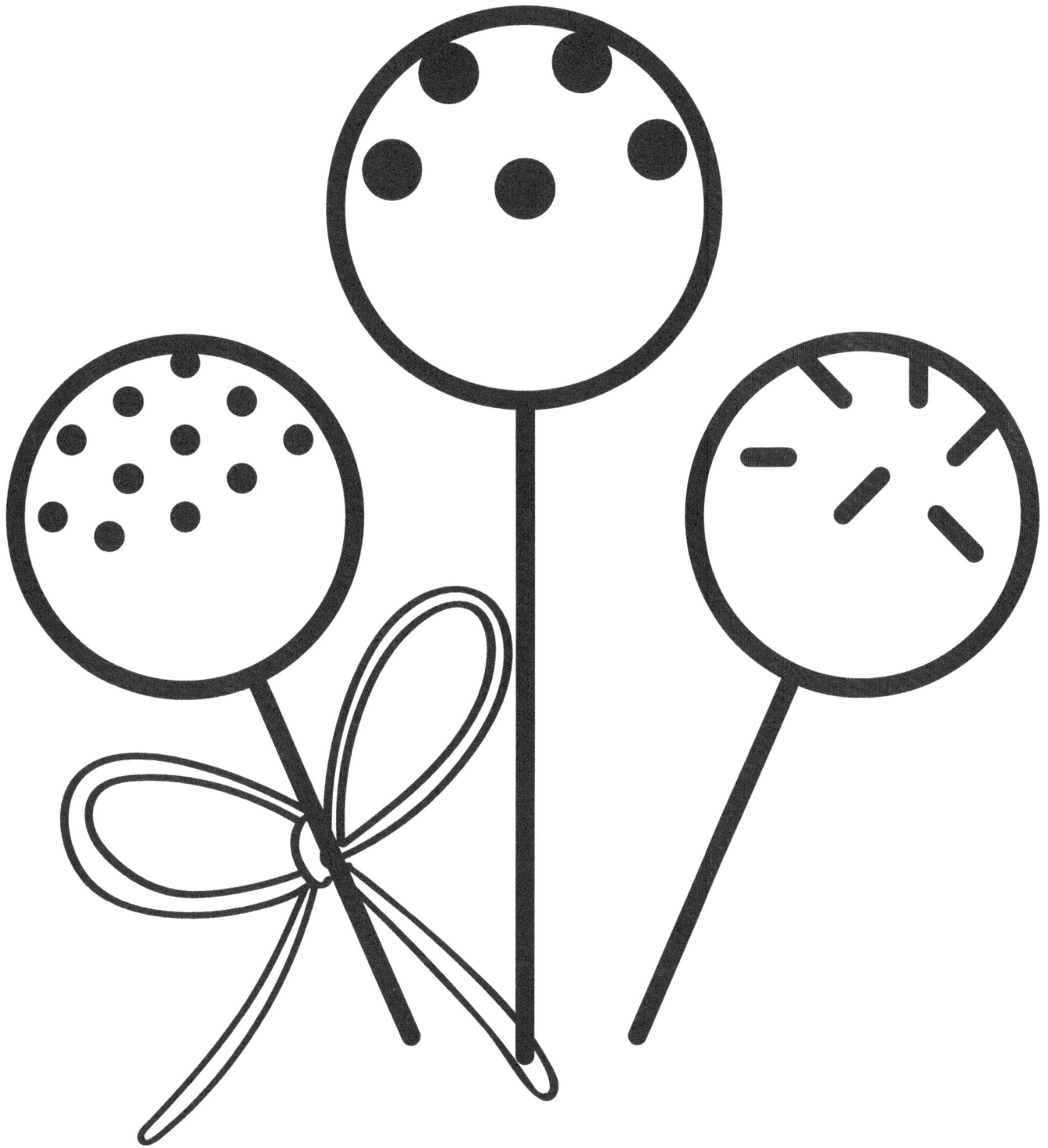

Cake Pop

Butterfly

Bunny

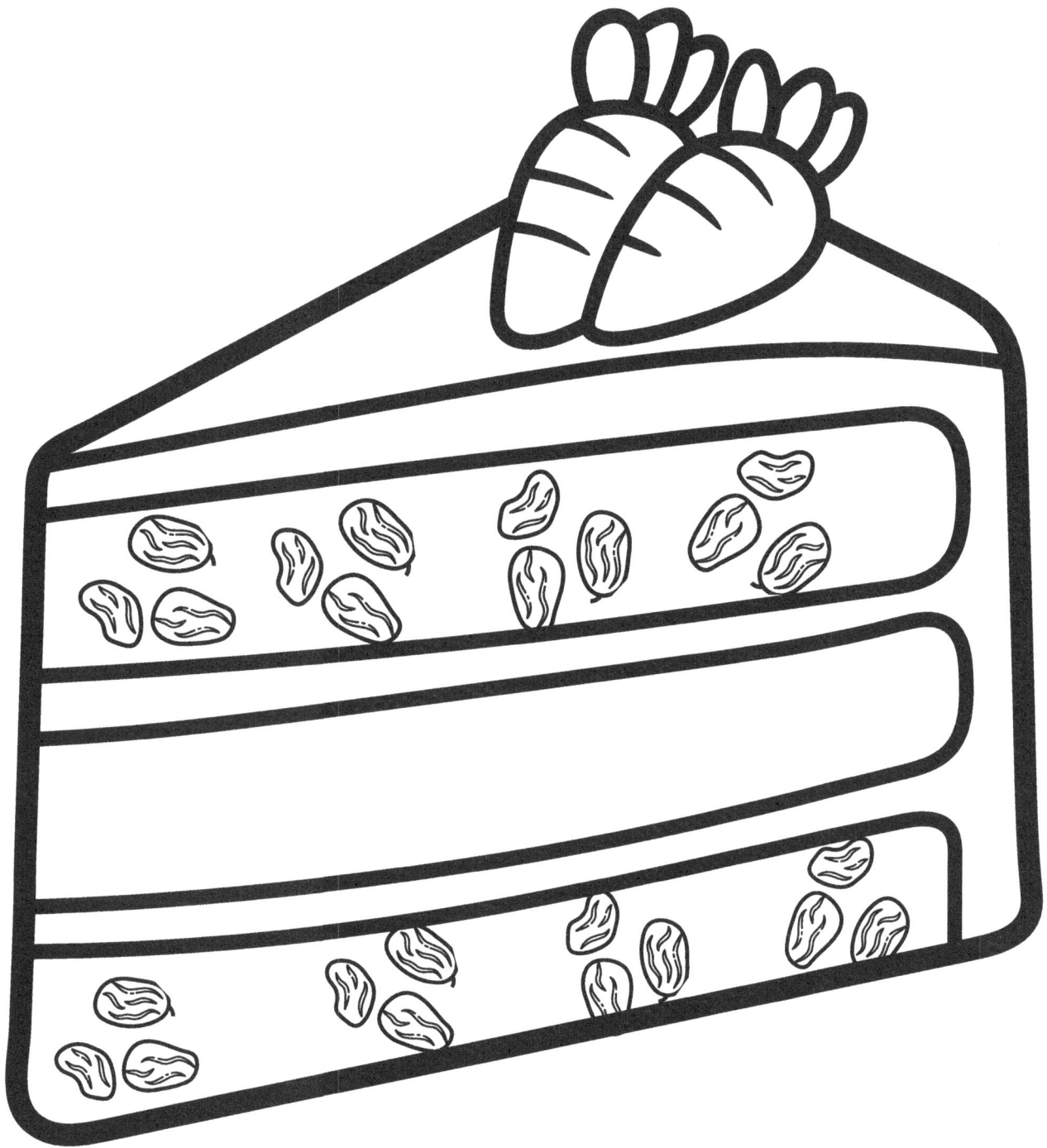

Cake

Ham

Dinner

I ♥ U

Love

Dress

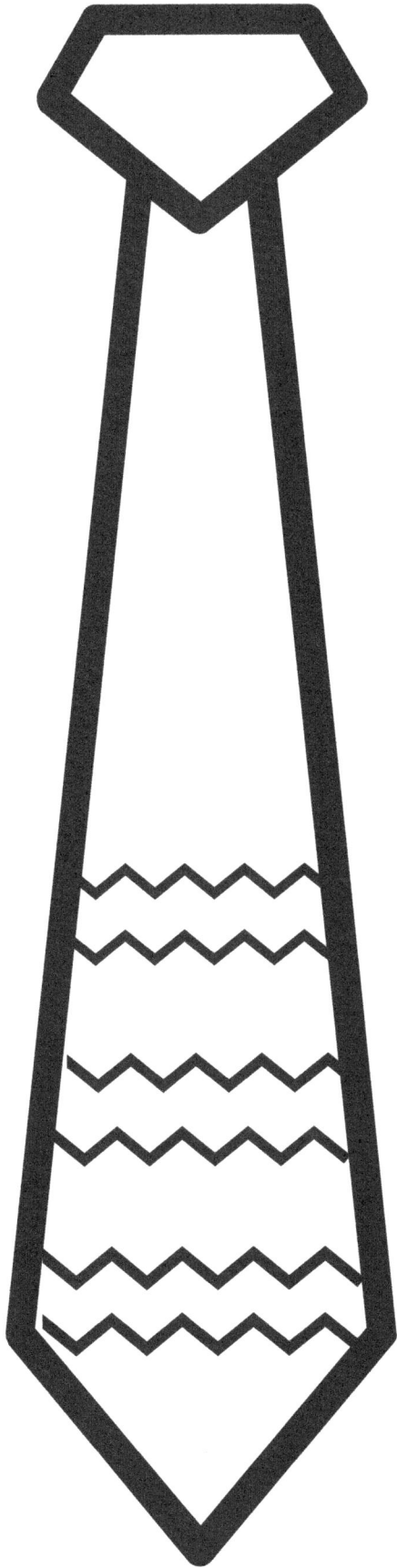

Tie

Church

Cross

Tomb

Happy

Easter!

If you liked this book, please leave a review! Follow us online & check out our other coloring books!

★★★★★

@CELEBRATINGTODAYPUBLISHING

Celebrating Today Publishing

CELEBRATING TODAY PUBLISHING

Made in the USA
Coppell, TX
10 April 2025